The SHIP Book

Michael Berenstain

David McKay Company, Inc.
New York

Library of Congress Cataloging in Publication Data

Berenstain, Michael.
The ship book.

SUMMARY: Briefly describes early sailing
vessels such as Egyptian reed boats, Viking
longships, Chinese junks, and American frigates.
1. Ships—History—Juvenile literature.
2. Navigation—History—Juvenile literature.
[1. Ships—History.   2. Navigation—History]
I. Title.
VM150.B46   387.2   77-14915
ISBN 0-679-20449-0

10 9 8 7 6 5 4 3
Manufactured in the United States of America

A simple floating log, paddled across a prehistoric stream, may well have been the beginning of all travel on water.

Hollowed out, the log became a dug-out canoe—the first boat.

If timber was scarce, the earliest people made other kinds of boats. In some places, animal hides were sewn onto branch frameworks to make round, tublike vessels.

In other places, long, narrow craft were made from bundles of hollow reeds.

About five thousand years ago, the Ancient Egyptians began building large reed boats, powered with both paddles and sails. These were the first vessels that could truly be called ships.

Later, they built great wooden sailing ships—often shaping and decorating them to look like the earlier reed boats. Although they were long and graceful, these ships were not very strong. Their hulls had to be strengthened with taut ropes passed from bow to stern.

The Egyptians used their ships mainly to sail up and down the River Nile. Only rarely did they venture into the open sea.

The Greeks and Romans were among the first peoples to make long sea voyages. They sailed on regular trade routes around the Mediterranean and the Indian Ocean.

Roman merchantmen, or trading ships, were rounded, seaworthy craft with small bow sails that made steering easier.

The warships of this period were called galleys. They were fast ships, long and low, propelled by banks of oars.

The rowers on Greek galleys were citizen-sailors who were proud of their tasks. But Roman galleys were manned by slaves and convicts who were often chained to their oars.

In battle, galleys were rowed forward at great speed. They rammed enemy ships—head-on—with their sharp, beaklike prows.

The eyes painted on their bows were thought to help the galleys "see"—a superstition still believed in some parts of the world.

After the fall of Rome, the greatest seafarers were the Vikings. These ruthless warriors from Scandinavia sailed south in their dragon-prowed longships to plunder the coasts of Europe.

They ranged far afield—east to Russia, south into the Mediterranean, and west to America—a discovery, however, soon forgotten.

The navies of other European countries could not compete with the Vikings. European ships were slow and clumsy—floating fortresses complete with turrets and knights in armor.

But, while the Vikings gradually abandoned their seafaring way of life, other countries relied on the sea more and more for trade and travel.

Soon, they began to build better and faster ships.

In the Mediterranean, two- and three-masted ships appeared. Rigged with triangular lateen sails, they were easier to steer and handle than one-masted, square-sailed ships.

In the 1400s, ships combining both kinds of sails came into use. Ships of this type were used by the Italian navigator Christopher Columbus when, in 1492, he attempted to reach China by sailing west. Instead, he rediscovered America.

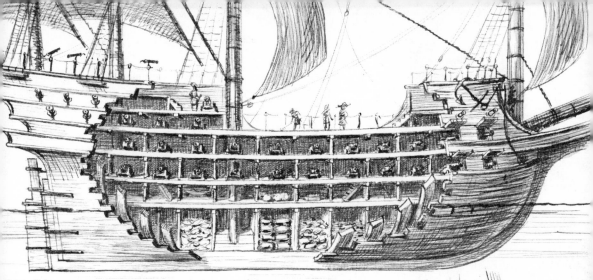

Columbus's ships were small and
frail, but soon, large, sturdy warships
were built. These great galleons had
many decks mounting heavy cannon,
and their crews often numbered in the
hundreds.

The greatest fleet of galleons ever assembled was the Spanish Armada. In 1588, the fleet set sail to launch an attack on England. But the outnumbered English fleet and a violent storm that struck without warning sent half of the Spanish ships to the bottom of the sea. Spain never fully recovered from this blow to her naval power.

While galleons and similar craft were the most widely used ships of their day, other types were also built.

Some countries used updated versions of the ancient galley, mounting heavy cannon instead of battering rams on their bows.

The Arab dhow was a lateen-rigged craft used on the trade routes of the Indian Ocean and Red Sea. Sturdy and reliable, dhows are still in use today.

The common ship of the Far East was the Chinese junk. Used for nearly every purpose—trade, war, and even piracy—these highly seaworthy craft had sails stiffened with bamboo poles, a feature helpful in controlling the ship.

Although these vessels were all fine sailing craft, they were not of the same quality as those built in the West. The future of the sailing ship lay in Europe and America.

During the 1700s, the sailing ship reached near perfection as a weapon of war. The two main classes of warship were the large, heavily armed ships of the line, and the smaller, faster frigates.

One of the most famous American frigates was the U.S.S. *Constitution*. Known as "Old Ironsides" because of her thick, oaken timbers, she was built in 1787 for use against Algerian pirates. But she reached her greatest moments of glory in action against the British during the War of 1812.

Shrouds   Mizzenmast   Mainmast

Spanker   Mainsail

1	Spar Deck	5	Wheel	9	Carronade
2	Gun Deck	6	Capstan	10	Cannon
3	Berth Deck	7	Ship's Boats	11	Anchor
4	Orlop Deck	8	Chimney	12	Cathead

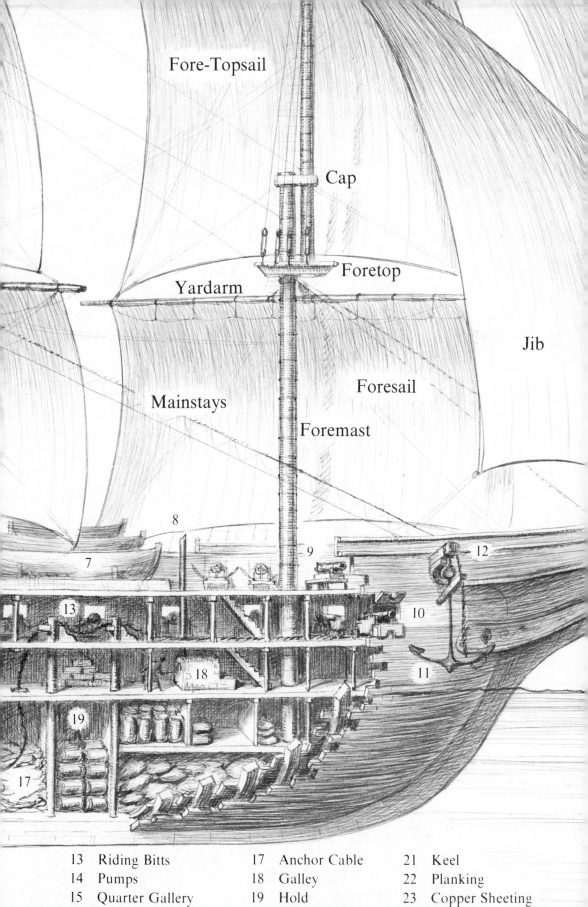

Fore-Topsail

Cap

Foretop

Yardarm

Jib

Mainstays

Foresail

Foremast

8

7

9

12

13

10

11

18

19

17

13	Riding Bitts	17	Anchor Cable	21	Keel
14	Pumps	18	Galley	22	Planking
15	Quarter Gallery	19	Hold	23	Copper Sheeting
16	Shot Lockers	20	Ribs	24	Rudder

Coming aboard the *Constitution,* as she was about to set sail, a new member of the crew reported to the officer of the watch before going about his duties.

When getting under way, the anchor was raised by turning the capstan—a large winch that wound up the anchor cable.

Next, the sails were set. To reach the upper rigging the crew climbed rope ladders to the mastheads.

High above the deck, the crew climbed out on the yardarms to set or take in sail.

When off duty, the crew went below to the gun deck. Normally peaceful and quiet, it became a scene of noise and confusion during battle. Then the cannon went off with immense roars, men ran back and forth with powder and shot, and thick smoke swirled in through the open gunports.

Below the gun deck was the berth deck where the crew slung their hammocks.

Also on the berth deck was the galley, the ship's kitchen. The galley oven was set in a sandbox to protect the ship from fire.

The lowest level of the ship was the hold. Supplies to last an entire voyage—water, food, spare sails, ropes, and wooden spars—were all stored here.

At the rear of the ship, on the level of the gun deck, was the captain's cabin. Here the captain plotted the ship's course and recorded the log (the ship's diary).

From the stern window the captain could look out over the ocean and back at the ship's wake marking a path through the water.

The *Constitution*'s fine design and highly trained crew made her a powerful ship of war. In forty-two battles she captured twenty ships, and she was never defeated. One of her most famous victories was over the British frigate *Guerrière*. In a battle lasting less than half an hour, she first dismasted, then sank the enemy vessel.

1. Loading

2. Ramming

Manning the Guns

3. Running-up

4. Ready

5. Fire!

During the 1800s, sailing ships were used for many purposes other than war. In America, one of the most important was whaling. Before the invention of kerosene, the best lamp fuel known was whale oil. To get it, whalers set out on voyages that often lasted years at a time.

Harpoons

Old-style Iron

Temple Toggle-iron (1848)

Killing-Lance

Matchstick Lock

Harpoons, or barbed spears, were used to "catch" the whale. When the whale was tired out from pulling the whale boat, it was killed with long, smooth-headed lances. The whale's blubber (a thick fat coating under its hide) was removed alongside the whale ship. The blubber was then taken on board and boiled down in huge kettles to make whale oil.

Bailer

Water trough

Oil-Keg

Improved types of ships continued to be built.

The Baltimore clipper was a small, fast craft much used in smuggling and the slave trade.

The six-masted schooner's simple, fore-and-aft rigging could be manned by a small crew.

The evolution of the sailing ship reached its peak with the China clippers. With their long, pointed hulls and immense spreads of sail, these great ships sailed all over the world. They carried tea from China, wool from Australia, and passengers across the Atlantic. During the California gold rush, they carried "forty-niners," or gold seekers, from New York to San Francisco by way of Cape Horn at the southern tip of South America. A clipper could make these voyages in less than half the time of other ships.

The clippers were built in a new way—with cast iron frameworks covered by wooden planking.

But despite their speed and strength, the days of the clippers were numbered. Steamships were steadily growing faster and more efficient. By 1900, the age of the sailing ship was over.

Today, sailing ships are mainly used for sport and recreation. They fight no battles, haul no cargo, discover no new lands or unknown seas.

But, despite this, they continue to play an important part in the modern world. For it is on full-rigged sailing ships, such as the U. S. Coast Guard's *Eagle,* that many of the world's naval officers are trained. Only on a vessel under sail can a sailor truly learn to understand ships and the sea.